Rory Margraf

I Know My Rights

A Children's Guide to the Bill of Rights and Individual Liberty

**Illustrated by
Andreea Mironiuc**

Illustrated by Andreea Mironiuc
www.andreeamironiuc.com

ISBN: 9781729436165

Dear Parents and Teachers,

At sixteen years old, I waived my Fourth Amendment rights when prompted by the authorities, answering questions and emptying my pockets. I did this, believing that I needed to comply and that I was doing the right thing, even though I was not guilty.

When telling this story to my mother less than thirty minutes later, I was scolded for ignoring my right to ask for Probable Cause or a Warrant based on evidence. While I had done nothing wrong, I could have implicated myself by answering incorrectly or forfeiting more information than necessary.

Having told this story many times over the years, I have found that reactions are often split, with some believing I did the right thing and others believing that my mother was correct in encouraging me to exercise my Fourth Amendment rights. What is concerning to most, I have found, is that, at sixteen years old, **I did not know the Fourth Amendment.**

It is with this experience in mind that I present this book.

The rights of every person, every man, woman, and child, are unalienable; though they are written as the law of the land, our rights transcend all of humanity's laws. They are tantamount to each individual living their most fulfilled life. The rights that we possess are not uniquely American, but rather natural rights that are possessed by all people.

*What is **uniquely American** is the explicit nature with which these rights must be acknowledged at all levels of government. As such, it is the responsibility of all Americans to exercise their rights daily, which means that the Bill of Rights must be a recurring study and part of regular discussion.*

*Learning our rights at **a young age** is an important step in growing to be a conscious citizen; one that will not only defend their own liberties, but those of their neighbors, friends, community, and strangers around the world.*

Our rights are not a partisan issue, but there are many interpretations of each of the first ten amendments, which means that debates must continue to take place and the laws that are meant to be a reflection of our rights will be challenged and will change throughout the course of each generation.

This book presents the original text of the first ten amendments of our Constitution – the Bill of Rights – followed by an explanation of how each amendment applies to our lives.

Each of the first ten amendments are far more nuanced than is often acknowledged. I implore you to **trust your children** to read and understand the text.

For younger readers, read along with them. Be prepared to discuss each amendment and answer any questions that they may have. It is important that you are as versed in the Bill of Rights as your children and are willing to discuss it openly with them.

Though they are children, their rights are no different than your own.

Yours in Liberty,
Rory

Growing up in the United States, you may sometimes hear someone say, "It's my right" or "I have rights" or "I know my rights."

But what is a right? Where do they come from? Are they gifts from our government or a natural part of being human?

Simply put, a right is a **natural entitlement**. Human beings have grown to understand a right as being a basic principle of society that grants us the ability to live our lives as we choose.

Our rights are a fundamental part of being human and guide our lives every day.

Imagine a city full of buildings. Each building must have a strong foundation so that it can stand tall and sturdy. Just like the buildings in a city, our country has a **foundation of rights** that allow us to live strong and sturdy lives.

Every person on US soil is guaranteed these rights by law.

Even someone visiting our country while on vacation, or going to school, or working, is protected by these rights.

The easiest way to sum up our rights is **"Life, Liberty, and Property."** These are the three basic things to which each person has a right.

This means that we have the right to live without fear of being harmed and that we are able to protect ourselves from physical assault. It also means that we have the responsibility to live peacefully.

We have the right to live freely, without anyone forcing us to live our lives in a way we don't wish.

And we have the right to own property, acquired honestly, and it can't be taken away from us without our permission.

Now, "Life, Liberty, and Property" may not seem like a lot at first, but these three things encompass everything in our lives, from ideas, to faith, to business, to what career you want, to what you put on your pizza!

This is why our Founding Fathers wrote the Bill of Rights!

The Bill of Rights is part of the United States Constitution.

After the Founding Fathers decided what kind of government we would have and how it would work, they had to make some rules that the government would have to follow.

In fact, the rules we put on the government are **the most important rules in the country**. The Bill of Rights ensures that the government cannot violate our rights.

Each law that Congress passes is subject to review by the people and it can be challenged in court. The Bill of Rights contains ten amendments to the Constitution, each defining the specific rights that we possess as citizens and human beings.

These were added to make sure that our new government didn't continue the tyranny of the British government that the colonists had rebelled against.

Let's start with Number One!

The First Amendment guarantees our right to be able to speak our minds, share ideas, and practice the religion of our choosing or none at all. It also guarantees that the government **will not favor** one religion over others.

We have the right to report the news to our communities and the right to protest or **come together to discuss ideas**. We can even demand change or criticize the government, so long as we do so **peacefully**.

With the First Amendment, we are guaranteed the right to **share any idea** you want, but that doesn't mean people have to listen to you or like what you say.

It's important to be **respectful** of the person you're talking to or about. Remember, part of being able to share all of the ideas we have with the world means that you might say something that someone doesn't like.

Or, someone might say something that you don't like.

Imagine all of these ideas being in a big marketplace. A **"Marketplace of Ideas."** You can choose what ideas you like and don't like and you can share your own along the way.

You can't force anyone to accept your ideas and beliefs, and they can't force you either. If you've got a good idea, share it and let others come to you naturally.

> **2.** *A well-regulated Militia, being necessary to the security of a free State, the right of the people to **keep and bear Arms**, shall not be infringed.*

The Second Amendment was written to ensure that every citizen can arm themselves. Because our country was formed from revolution, the Founding Fathers believed that if everyone owned a firearm, we could protect ourselves from future tyranny.

The United States also has a standing military, even in times of peace. Some of the Founders were worried this meant that we could face future oppression through the use of military force. So we must be able to protect our liberty.

We also have **the right to protect ourselves, our families, and our property.** Firearms are one of the many ways that we can do this. They can also be used for hunting and for sport.

Just like the First Amendment, the Second Amendment takes a lot of **responsibility**. Firearms require a lot of training and experience to own and operate safely, just like driving a car.

They should always be treated with **respect**, proper supervision, and care.

Many folks don't like firearms or just don't want to own one and that's perfectly fine. Just because you have the right to own something doesn't mean that you have the obligation.

It's all about **personal choice**; living your life in your own way. If owning a firearm isn't a part of your life, that's absolutely okay.

Many people are still debating whether anyone should own a firearm at all. It's been a long debate and will probably go on for years. That's why the First Amendment is so important. Everyone has an opinion and has the right to share it and discuss it with others.

We just have to remember to be **mindful of other people's beliefs**. We don't have to agree with each other, but we should always respect each other.

3. No Soldier shall, in time of peace be quartered in any house, without the **Consent** of the Owner, nor in time of war, but in a manner to be prescribed by law.

During, and long before, the Revolutionary War, it was common for soldiers to live in private citizens' homes, **without permission** of the homeowner.

Even in times of peace, soldiers were allowed to live among civilians, and you could not object.

The Third Amendment isn't talked about a lot today but, it does help to establish the **boundaries** of our relationship with the government.

This includes our politicians, law enforcement, and the military.

Our Founders wanted it to be clear that an individual's property is their own and it cannot be used or taken away without our permission.

Think of it this way: *what would you call it if someone used or borrowed something without your permission?*

It'd be stealing! No one is allowed to steal from you, including any part of the government.

Which brings us to the Fourth Amendment!

*4. The right of the people **to be secure** in their persons, houses, papers, and effects, against unreasonable searches and seizures, shall not be violated, and no Warrants shall issue, but upon **Probable Cause**, supported by Oath or affirmation, and particularly describing the place to be searched, and the persons or things to be seized.*

If you've ever seen anyone pulled over on the road by a police officer or stopped on the sidewalk, or have watched a detective show, you've seen the Fourth Amendment in action.

This is part of what's called **"Due Process."** Officers and detectives must have a reason to stop you, ask you questions, have you empty your pockets, search your property, or even have you step out of your car!

Much of the time, the officer must have written permission from a judge to arrest a citizen or search their property. That permission has to be based on evidence and it has to state what can be searched. That's called a **"Warrant."**

Sometimes, a police officer might witness a crime or have a reasonable suspicion that a crime has taken place or is about to, in which case, they don't necessarily need a Warrant. That's called **"Probable Cause,"** which is still based on evidence.

The Fourth Amendment was written because of a practice used in the Colonies and even Great Britain. Authorities could obtain a **"General Warrant,"** which allowed them to search a person and their property at any time, without a reason. Some officials used that as a way of going after people they didn't like. Just because you don't get along with someone doesn't mean they don't have the same rights as you.

You're growing up with a lot of new technology and the world is more connected than ever! Today, the government has the ability listen to phone calls, read our emails and text messages, see what websites we visit, and much more.

While our Founding Fathers could never have imagined this new technology when the Fourth Amendment was written, it doesn't change the fact that these things are protected, just like any other property.

Sometimes, you might hear stories of persons refusing to answer questions or not allowing their property to be searched. **Saying "no" to a police officer isn't wrong.** In fact, it's often the right thing to do! We want to be as helpful as we can, but we still have our rights and it's important that we maintain their integrity.

If an officer starts asking you questions or asks to search your property, first ask for a reason. If they don't have one, say "no" politely and walk away. If they have a reason, or "Probable Cause," you should make sure you have a parent with you before you speak to them further.

Be polite, but be firm. Never be afraid to use the Fourth Amendment. Even if you are under arrest, you still have rights.

*5. **No person shall be held to answer for a capital, or otherwise infamous crime, unless on a presentment or indictment of a Grand Jury**, except in cases arising in the land or naval forces, or in the Militia, when in actual service in time of War or public danger; nor shall any person be subject for the same offence to be twice put in jeopardy of life or limb; nor shall be compelled in any criminal case to be a witness against himself, nor be deprived of life, liberty, or property, without **Due Process of law**; nor shall private property be taken for public use, without just compensation.*

The Fourth, Fifth, Sixth, Seventh, and Eighth Amendments are all part of "Due Process" and are the longest of the ten.

Let's take it piece by piece.

The first part of the Fifth Amendment refers to a **"capital or infamous crime"** and a **"Grand Jury."** When a person is facing serious charges in Federal Court, a "Grand Jury" must review the evidence and decide if the person can be charged at all.

The United States is the only country to use Grand Juries and it isn't considered necessary in order to charge someone with a crime.

12

Whether a person is charged with a crime by a Grand Jury or without, the government must have **enough evidence** to prove the accused's guilt.

The next part refers to "Double Jeopardy," which means that **a person cannot face trial for the same crime twice**. If the government is not able to prove a person's guilt in the first trial, a person cannot be forced to face a second trial. If they have been found innocent, then they are free to return to their life. There are some rare exceptions to this, but overall, it stands as is.

The next part might sound familiar to you. Have you ever heard of someone "taking" or "pleading the Fifth?" This means that an accused person may choose not to testify in a trial, if they believe that there is a chance that they could incriminate themselves.

In other words, a person may say something under oath that could prove their guilt, whether they intended to say it or were tricked by a question.

The "Supreme Court" has also ruled that choosing not to answer for this reason, or any reason, is not proof of guilt. **It's natural to refuse answering questions if we could prove our own guilt.** The government cannot force you to answer questions at trial.

Remember "Life, Liberty, and Property?"

The Fifth Amendment protects these three things until a person is found guilty or innocent. **A person may not be harmed; a person may not have their rights taken from them; a person may not have their property taken from them until after their guilt has been proven and if it is necessary.**

Outside of court, the government may not take a person's property without compensating them properly.

If the government were to take your home, they must pay you fairly for it. This is called "**Eminent Domain**" and, while it is in the Fifth Amendment and is widely practiced, there are many that wish to see the practice end. Even though you are compensated, you may not want your property taken at all.

Let's take a deep breath and move on to the Sixth Amendment.

We're halfway there!

6. *In all criminal prosecutions, the accused shall enjoy the right to a* **speedy** *and* **public** *trial, by an impartial jury of the State and district wherein the crime shall have been committed, which district shall have been previously ascertained by law, and* **to be informed** *of the nature and cause of the accusation;* **to be confronted** *with the witnesses against him;* **to have compulsory process for obtaining witnesses in his favor,** *and* **to have the Assistance of Counsel for his defense.**

The Sixth Amendment refers to the actual trial process.

Each of us has a right to a speedy trial; it wouldn't be fair to arrest someone and then leave that person in prison for months or even years!

A jury is selected at random from the community and they are the ones who decide if someone is innocent or guilty.

When a person is arrested, they must be told **the crime of which they are accused** and they have **the right to face their accuser and ask them questions during the trial.**

You also have **the right to defend yourself**, present your own evidence and witnesses, and have a lawyer help you make your case.

In fact, if you don't have enough money to pay a lawyer, the government must provide one to help you.

One thing to remember is that when the government charges you with a crime, it's the government's job to prove it in court. This is called the **"Burden of Proof."**

It's not your job to prove your innocence, it's the government's job to prove your guilt.

Remember, in the United States, a person must always be thought of as innocent until they are found guilty by the jury.

Just because a person is arrested does not necessarily mean they are guilty. It's up to the government to prove it; until then, they must be thought of as innocent.

7. *In Suits at common law, where the value in controversy shall exceed twenty dollars,* **the right of trial by jury shall be preserved,** *and no fact tried by a jury, shall be otherwise reexamined in any Court of the United States, than according to the rules of the common law.*

Now, twenty dollars might not seem like a lot of money, but, you have to remember that the Seventh Amendment was written in 1789.

That's over **two hundred** years ago! Twenty dollars was worth a lot more than it is today. Twenty dollars only fifty years ago was worth a lot more!

The Seventh Amendment is rarely enforced, and usually only at the Federal level.

Let's pretend that I offered to mow your lawn for twenty five dollars and you agreed, but after I finished, you refused to pay me. I could file a lawsuit to have the court settle the dispute.

If it was in a Federal court, I could request that a jury decide who was right, just like a jury decides if someone is guilty or innocent. But, if the lawsuit was in a State court, like your local courthouse, it would most likely be a judge that decides, instead of a jury.

It's still very important to remember, but most lawsuits are settled by a judge and not a jury.

Let's look at number Eight!

*8. **Excessive bail** shall not be required, nor excessive fines imposed, nor cruel and unusual punishments inflicted.*

The Eighth Amendment is very short, but it's just as important as the rest! Let's pretend that you've been arrested and the judge assigns a **"Bail,"** which is a sum of money that you may pay to be granted temporary freedom until your trial begins.

Remember the Sixth Amendment? You have the right to make a defense in court. It's much easier to make a defense if you're free to stay at home, meet with your lawyer, talk to witnesses, and conduct your own investigation.

If you are unable to pay your bail, you may have to stay in jail. You can still make a defense, but it's much harder.

Bail cannot be used as a punishment prior to a person's trial. It must be based reasonably upon the individual and the crime of which they are accused.

Even today, many people are unable to afford bail and must sit in jail for months or even years until their trial begins! They could lose their job, their car, even their home while they wait!

Many people today are fighting to make sure that bail is fair for everyone and they are using the Eighth Amendment as the reason why.

Unfair bail is considered **"Unconstitutional."** In other words, it's a violation of a person's rights.

Now, some crimes don't require being sent to jail. Your punishment may be simply paying some money to the government, which is called a **"Fine"**. But, just like bail, if fines are too high, someone who can't afford it could be put in jail. And they could lose their job or property again.

Punishments cannot be "cruel or unusual." You may be a criminal, but you still have rights. A punishment cannot be humiliating, or painful, or dangerous. Some prisons used to let prisoners go hungry or made them sit in the sun all day or forced them into a dark jail cell with no one to talk to for months and years. **Punishment is not about revenge.**

Punishment is about justice for the victim. Restoring what was lost is far better than making someone suffer. We want to prevent crime, but we don't want to hurt people and we certainly don't want to violate their rights.

Someone who makes a mistake must make it right, but we must trust that they won't do it again. **A community is based on trust**, even trust in those who do something wrong.

> *9.* *The enumeration in the Constitution, of certain rights, shall not be construed to **deny or disparage others** retained by the people.*

Just like the Eighth Amendment, the Ninth Amendment is extremely important, as short as it is.

The Founding Fathers were worried that listing our rights would mean that no other rights would be protected. The government could make laws that restricted other rights, simply because we didn't write them down!

Remember, "Life, Liberty, and Property."

You have the right to learn a new language, play an instrument, learn new skills, have a certain job or even create a brand new industry! **No one can stop you from living the life you want**, especially the government.

The Founders made it clear that just because it's not written in the Constitution, doesn't mean that it's not a right. That's why we're able to add additional amendments to the Constitution. There are twenty seven amendments altogether, and we can always add more. The Bill of Rights is only the first ten!

Some of the other amendments are about the structure of government. The Twenty Second Amendment limits the President to only two terms, which means he or she can't be elected more than twice. The Twenty Fifth Amendment is about the "Line of Succession," which talks about what to do if the President is no longer able to serve.

Others reaffirm the rights of the people. The Thirteenth Amendment makes it illegal to force anyone into slavery. You can't own another human being.

Part of "Life, Liberty, and Property" is something called "**Self-Ownership.**" **Only you are in control of your life.** That doesn't mean we shouldn't listen to our parents or our teachers, but we have to be wise enough to know when these rights are being violated.

You can always work for someone voluntarily and agree on payment, that's called a "Job," but no one can force you, especially not the government.

Another important amendment is the Nineteenth Amendment, which made it clear that a person's gender should not keep them from voting. Before this Amendment was passed in 1920, women were not allowed to vote. Women possess the same natural rights as men and the Constitution was changed to make that clear.

Who you are as a person, no matter your age, gender, race, religion, or ethnicity, does not change your rights.

To learn more, you can find the entire Constitution at your local bookstore or library or online. You can even find copies small enough to fit in your pocket or download a copy on your phone, so you can always have it with you.

All twenty seven amendments are at the end of this book too! You can read each one and discuss them with your parents and teachers, even your siblings and friends.

It's very important that everyone learns their rights.

> **10.** *The powers not delegated to the United States by the Constitution, nor prohibited by it to the States, **are reserved** to the States respectively, or to the people.*

The Tenth Amendment has to do with "States' Rights."

Some of the Founders were worried that by listing our rights as a people, the Federal Government would appear to have more power than actually given to it by the Constitution.

So the Tenth Amendment was written to make clear that the government is bound by the rules of the Bill of Rights and the powers granted to it by the Constitution. Any power not granted to the government is a matter for each individual state to decide on. That's why each state has its own Constitution.

The most important job of the government is **to protect our rights as a free people**.

The most important job of the people is to ensure that **the government doesn't violate our rights**.

People interpret our rights differently, and that's okay, but we can all agree that we have a duty to protect the individual's rights first.

This means that the government will not have the power to do certain things. But each of us, as individuals and communities, do possess the power to create value and prosperity for each other, so long as we willing.

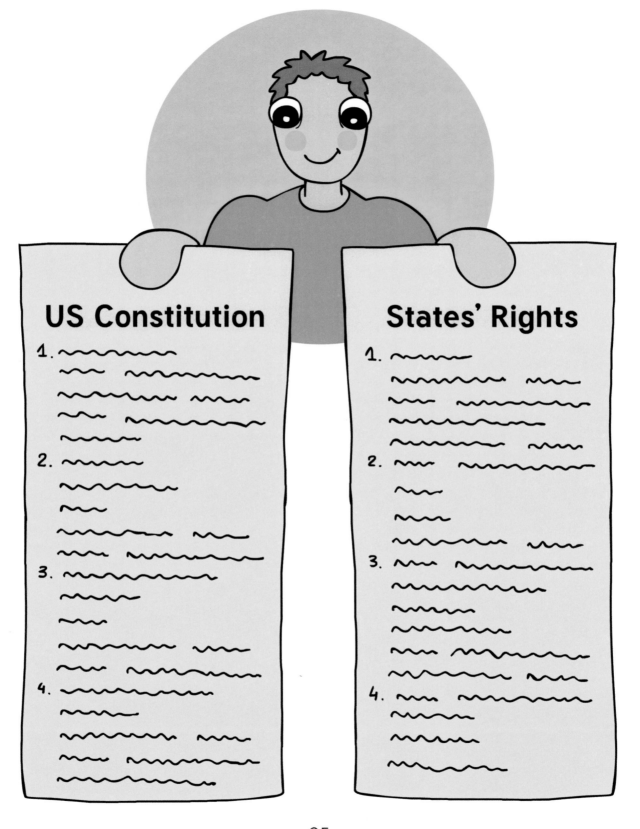

Some people make the mistake of believing that our rights were given to us by the government. That's not true at all.

You see, the government didn't give us these rights or allow us to have them; these are "**Human Rights**." We have these rights just by being born.

Some people believe that these rights were given to us by God and many others believe that we began to understand them as we evolved as a society. For others, it's a little bit of both. No matter what you believe, **these rights are a natural part of being human.**

But not everyone is able to express their rights; there are governments around the world that enforce laws that would be considered unconstitutional in the United States. Remember, we all possess these rights, so it is important that the government is kept from overstepping its authority.

That's why we have the Bill of Rights. It is a way of listing out what is natural for human beings and making sure the government doesn't restrict or oppress our lives. Even today, the United States is one of the few countries in the entire world that has a Bill of Rights.

Many people live in countries where they can be punished for saying or writing something the government doesn't like. They are punished for having a different religion or no religion at all. Some people are thought less of for being a different gender or different race and are treated unequally by the government. Many countries have horrible punishments for criminals and have little or no due process.

Even our country has made mistakes and we still make some today. **That's why it's important that we always have the courage to speak out when it's necessary.**

It's up to the people to assert and defend their rights.

You may be wondering, *"If we all have these rights and can live our lives however we want, how can we live together with so many different ideas, beliefs, and lifestyles?"*

The most important thing we must remember in our relationship with other people is **"Consent."**

Whether you're buying or borrowing something, or interacting with other people, the individuals involved must agree. It's okay to have a job and work for somebody else, as long as you agree to do it. It's okay to acquire someone else's property, as long as they agree to give it to you. You cannot make others obey you and they cannot make you obey them.

Think about when you go to the store with your parents. The groceries belong to the store owner and they set the prices. As long as your parents agree to pay that price, they can take the groceries home. If your parents don't like the prices, they can go to another store, but they can't take the groceries with them. This is called **"Voluntaryism."**

As long as a person gives their consent, it's not a violation of their rights. If they don't, then you can't take what's not yours. We can peacefully agree or disagree, but we must respect each other's wishes.

You have to remember, there are so many choices out there, that when we don't like something, we can choose something else. If you don't like a game, there are other games out there to play. If you don't like a book, there are millions of other books to read.

Remember the Marketplace of Ideas? There's always something else out there. It's when we're not given a choice that it becomes a problem. If we don't have a choice to do something else, or buy something else, or work somewhere else, then your rights are being violated and that's not acceptable in the United States or anywhere in the world!

This is a lot to remember and that's why we always have to study our rights. Even adults forget from time to time. Some adults don't know their rights at all!

It's important that we keep discussing them, as a regular part of our lives. Talk to your parents and teachers, your siblings and friends.

Pay attention to your community, listen to what your elected officials are saying and talk about what that means for your rights.

Having these rights, as a person, means that we also have a duty to maintain their integrity and protect them. **That's how we learn to live peacefully.** The older you get, and the more you pay attention, the more complicated it will feel. But, as long as you keep studying and exercising your rights every day, it will come naturally to you.

And now you know your rights!

The Amendments to the Constitution of the United States

First Amendment
Congress shall make no law respecting an establishment of religion, or prohibiting the free exercise thereof; or abridging the freedom of speech, or of the press; or the right of the people peaceably to assemble, and to petition the Government for a redress of grievances.

Second Amendment
A well-regulated Militia, being necessary to the security of a free State, the right of the people to keep and bear Arms, shall not be infringed.

Third Amendment
No Soldier shall, in time of peace be quartered in any house, without the Consent of the Owner, nor in time of war, but in a manner to be prescribed by law.

Fourth Amendment
The right of the people to be secure in their persons, houses, papers, and effects, against unreasonable searches and seizures, shall not be violated, and no Warrants shall issue, but upon Probable Cause, supported by Oath or affirmation, and particularly describing the place to be searched, and the persons or things to be seized.

Fifth Amendment
No person shall be held to answer for a capital, or otherwise infamous crime, unless on a presentment or indictment of a Grand Jury, except in cases arising in the land or naval forces, or in the Militia, when in actual service in time of War or public danger; nor shall any person be subject for the same offence to be twice put in jeopardy of life or limb; nor shall be compelled in any criminal case to be a witness against himself, nor be deprived of life, liberty, or property, without Due Process of law; nor shall private property be taken for public use, without just compensation.

Sixth Amendment
In all criminal prosecutions, the accused shall enjoy the right to a speedy and public trial, by an impartial jury of the State and district wherein the crime shall have been committed, which district shall have been previously ascertained by law, and to be informed of the nature and cause of the accusation; to be confronted with the witnesses against him; to have compulsory process for obtaining witnesses in his favor, and to have the Assistance of Counsel for his defense.

Seventh Amendment
In Suits at common law, where the value in controversy shall exceed twenty dollars, the right of trial by jury shall be preserved, and no fact tried by a jury, shall be otherwise re-examined in any Court of the United States, than according to the rules of the common law.

Eighth Amendment
Excessive bail shall not be required, nor excessive fines imposed, nor cruel and unusual punishments inflicted.

Ninth Amendment
The enumeration in the Constitution, of

certain rights, shall not be construed to deny or disparage others retained by the people.

Tenth Amendment

The powers not delegated to the United States by the Constitution, nor prohibited by it to the States, are reserved to the States respectively, or to the people.

Eleventh Amendment

The Judicial power of the United States shall not be construed to extend to any suit in law or equity, commenced or prosecuted against one of the United States by Citizens of another State, or by Citizens or Subjects of any Foreign State.

Twelfth Amendment

The Electors shall meet in their respective states and vote by ballot for President and Vice-President, one of whom, at least, shall not be an inhabitant of the same state with themselves; they shall name in their ballots the person voted for as President, and in distinct ballots the person voted for as Vice-President, and they shall make distinct lists of all persons voted for as President, and of all persons voted for as Vice-President, and of the number of votes for each, which lists they shall sign and certify, and transmit sealed to the seat of the government of the United States, directed to the President of the Senate; -- the President of the Senate shall, in the presence of the Senate and House of Representatives, open all the certificates and the votes shall then be counted; -- The person having the greatest number of votes for President, shall be the President, if such number be a majority of the whole number of Electors appointed; and if no person have such majority, then from the persons having the highest numbers not exceeding three on the list of those voted for as President, the House of Representatives shall choose immediately, by ballot, the President. But in choosing the President, the votes shall be taken by states, the representation from each state having one vote; a quorum for this purpose shall consist of a member or members from two-thirds of the states, and a majority of all the states shall be necessary to a choice. And if the House of Representatives shall not choose a President whenever the right of choice shall devolve upon them, before the fourth day of March next following, then the Vice-President shall act as President, as in case of the death or other constitutional disability of the President. --* The person having the greatest number of votes as Vice-President, shall be the Vice-President, if such number be a majority of the whole number of Electors appointed, and if no person have a majority, then from the two highest numbers on the list, the Senate shall choose the Vice-President; a quorum for the purpose shall consist of two-thirds of the whole number of Senators, and a majority of the whole number shall be necessary to a choice. But no person constitutionally ineligible to the office of President shall be eligible to that of Vice-President of the United States.

*Superseded by section 3 of the 20th amendment.

Thirteenth Amendment

Section 1.

Neither slavery nor involuntary

servitude, except as a punishment for crime whereof the party shall have been duly convicted, shall exist within the United States, or any place subject to their jurisdiction.

Section 2.

Congress shall have power to enforce this article by appropriate legislation.

Fourteenth Amendment

Section 1.

All persons born or naturalized in the United States, and subject to the jurisdiction thereof, are citizens of the United States and of the State wherein they reside. No State shall make or enforce any law which shall abridge the privileges or immunities of citizens of the United States; nor shall any State deprive any person of life, liberty, or property, without Due Process of law; nor deny to any person within its jurisdiction the equal protection of the laws.

Section 2.

Representatives shall be apportioned among the several States according to their respective numbers, counting the whole number of persons in each State, excluding Indians not taxed. But when the right to vote at any election for the choice of electors for President and Vice-President of the United States, Representatives in Congress, the Executive and Judicial officers of a State, or the members of the Legislature thereof, is denied to any of the male inhabitants of such State, being twenty-one years of age,* and citizens of the United States, or in any way abridged, except for participation in rebellion, or other crime, the basis of representation therein shall be reduced in the proportion which the number of such male citizens shall bear to the whole number of male citizens twenty-one years of age in such State.

Section 3.

No person shall be a Senator or Representative in Congress, or elector of President and Vice-President, or hold any office, civil or military, under the United States, or under any State, who, having previously taken an oath, as a member of Congress, or as an officer of the United States, or as a member of any State legislature, or as an executive or judicial officer of any State, to support the Constitution of the United States, shall have engaged in insurrection or rebellion against the same, or given aid or comfort to the enemies thereof. But Congress may by a vote of two-thirds of each House, remove such disability.

Section 4.

The validity of the public debt of the United States, authorized by law, including debts incurred for payment of pensions and bounties for services in suppressing insurrection or rebellion, shall not be questioned. But neither the United States nor any State shall assume or pay any debt or obligation incurred in aid of insurrection or rebellion against the United States, or any claim for the loss or emancipation of any slave; but all such debts, obligations and claims shall be held illegal and void.

Section 5.

The Congress shall have the power to enforce, by appropriate legislation, the provisions of this article.

*Changed by section 1 of the 26th amendment.

Fifteenth Amendment
Section 1.

The right of citizens of the United States to vote shall not be denied or abridged by the United States or by any State on account of race, color, or previous condition of servitude--

Section 2.

The Congress shall have the power to enforce this article by appropriate legislation.

Sixteenth Amendment

The Congress shall have power to lay and collect taxes on incomes, from whatever source derived, without apportionment among the several States, and without regard to any census or enumeration.

Seventeenth Amendment

The Senate of the United States shall be composed of two Senators from each State, elected by the people thereof, for six years; and each Senator shall have one vote. The electors in each State shall have the qualifications requisite for electors of the most numerous branch of the State legislatures. When vacancies happen in the representation of any State in the Senate, the executive authority of such State shall issue writs of election to fill such vacancies: Provided, That the legislature of any State may empower the executive thereof to make temporary appointments until the people fill the vacancies by election as the legislature may direct. This amendment shall not be so construed as to affect the election or term of any Senator chosen before it becomes valid as part of the Constitution.

Eighteenth Amendment
Section 1.

After one year from the ratification of this article the manufacture, sale, or transportation of intoxicating liquors within, the importation thereof into, or the exportation thereof from the United States and all territory subject to the jurisdiction thereof for beverage purposes is hereby prohibited.

Section 2.

The Congress and the several States shall have concurrent power to enforce this article by appropriate legislation.

Section 3.

This article shall be inoperative unless it shall have been ratified as an amendment to the Constitution by the legislatures of the several States, as provided in the Constitution, within seven years from the date of the submission hereof to the States by the Congress.

Nineteenth Amendment

The right of citizens of the United States to vote shall not be denied or abridged by the United States or by any State on account of sex.

Congress shall have power to enforce this article by appropriate legislation.

Twentieth Amendment
Section 1.

The terms of the President and the Vice President shall end at noon on the 20th day of January, and the terms of Senators and Representatives at noon on the 3d day of January, of the years in which such terms would have ended if this article had not been ratified; and the terms of their successors shall then begin.

Section 2.

The Congress shall assemble at least once in every year, and such meeting shall begin at noon on the 3rd day of January, unless they shall by law appoint a different day.

Section 3.

If, at the time fixed for the beginning of the term of the President, the President elect shall have died, the Vice President elect shall become President. If a President shall not have been chosen before the time fixed for the beginning of his term, or if the President elect shall have failed to qualify, then the Vice President elect shall act as President until a President shall have qualified; and the Congress may by law provide for the case wherein neither a President elect nor a Vice President shall have qualified, declaring who shall then act as President, or the manner in which one who is to act shall be selected, and such person shall act accordingly until a President or Vice President shall have qualified.

Section 4.

The Congress may by law provide for the case of the death of any of the persons from whom the House of Representatives may choose a President whenever the right of choice shall have devolved upon them, and for the case of the death of any of the persons from whom the Senate may choose a Vice President whenever the right of choice shall have devolved upon them.

Section 5.

Sections 1 and 2 shall take effect on the 15th day of October following the ratification of this article.

Section 6.

This article shall be inoperative unless it shall have been ratified as an amendment to the Constitution by the legislatures of three-fourths of the several States within seven years from the date of its submission.

Twenty First Amendment

Section 1.

The eighteenth article of amendment to the Constitution of the United States is hereby repealed.

Section 2.

The transportation or importation into any State, Territory, or Possession of the United States for delivery or use therein of intoxicating liquors, in violation of the laws thereof, is hereby prohibited.

Section 3.

This article shall be inoperative unless it shall have been ratified as an amendment to the Constitution by conventions in the several States, as provided in the Constitution, within seven years from the date of the submission hereof to the States by the Congress.

Twenty Second Amendment

Section 1.

No person shall be elected to the office of the President more than twice, and no person who has held the office of President, or acted as President, for more than two years of a term to which some other person was elected President shall be elected to the office of President more than once. But this Article shall not apply to any person holding the office of President when this Article was proposed by Congress, and shall not prevent any person who may be holding the office of President, or acting as President, during the term within which this Article becomes operative from holding the office of President or acting as President during the remainder of such term.

Section 2.
This article shall be inoperative unless it shall have been ratified as an amendment to the Constitution by the legislatures of three-fourths of the several States within seven years from the date of its submission to the States by the Congress.

Twentieth Third Amendment
Section 1.
The District constituting the seat of Government of the United States shall appoint in such manner as Congress may direct:
A number of electors of President and Vice President equal to the whole number of Senators and Representatives in Congress to which the District would be entitled if it were a State, but in no event more than the least populous State; they shall be in addition to those appointed by the States, but they shall be considered, for the purposes of the election of President and Vice President, to be electors appointed by a State; and they shall meet in the District and perform such duties as provided by the twelfth article of amendment.
Section 2.
The Congress shall have power to enforce this article by appropriate legislation.

Twenty Fourth Amendment
Section 1.
The right of citizens of the United States to vote in any primary or other election for President or Vice President, for electors for President or Vice President, or for Senator or Representative in Congress, shall not be denied or abridged by the United States or any State by reason of failure to pay poll tax or other tax.

Section 2.
The Congress shall have power to enforce this article by appropriate legislation.

Twenty Fifth Amendment
Section 1.
In case of the removal of the President from office or of his death or resignation, the Vice President shall become President.
Section 2.
Whenever there is a vacancy in the office of the Vice President, the President shall nominate a Vice President who shall take office upon confirmation by a majority vote of both Houses of Congress.
Section 3.
Whenever the President transmits to the President pro tempore of the Senate and the Speaker of the House of Representatives his written declaration that he is unable to discharge the powers and duties of his office, and until he transmits to them a written declaration to the contrary, such powers and duties shall be discharged by the Vice President as Acting President.
Section 4.
Whenever the Vice President and a majority of either the principal officers of the executive departments or of such other body as Congress may by law provide, transmit to the President pro tempore of the Senate and the Speaker of the House of Representatives their written declaration that the President is unable to discharge the powers and duties of his office, the Vice President shall immediately assume the powers and duties of the office as Acting President. Thereafter, when the President transmits to the President pro tempore of the

Senate and the Speaker of the House of Representatives his written declaration that no inability exists, he shall resume the powers and duties of his office unless the Vice President and a majority of either the principal officers of the executive department or of such other body as Congress may by law provide, transmit within four days to the President pro tempore of the Senate and the Speaker of the House of Representatives their written declaration that the President is unable to discharge the powers and duties of his office. Thereupon Congress shall decide the issue, assembling within forty-eight hours for that purpose if not in session. If the Congress, within twenty-one days after receipt of the latter written declaration, or, if Congress is not in session, within twenty-one days after Congress is required to assemble, determines by two-thirds vote of both Houses that the President is unable to discharge the powers and duties of his office, the Vice President shall continue to discharge the same as Acting President; otherwise, the President shall resume the powers and duties of his office.

Twenty Sixth Amendment

Section 1.

The right of citizens of the United States, who are eighteen years of age or older, to vote shall not be denied or abridged by the United States or by any State on account of age.

Section 2.

The Congress shall have power to enforce this article by appropriate legislation.

Twenty Seventh Amendment

No law, varying the compensation for the services of the Senators and Representatives, shall take effect, until an election of representatives shall have intervened.

Glossary

Bail – The temporary release of an accused person awaiting trial, sometimes on condition that a sum of money be lodged to guarantee their appearance in court

Burden of Proof – The obligation to offer evidence that the court or jury could reasonably believe, in support of a contention, failing which the case will be lost

Consent – To permit, approve, or agree

Double Jeopardy – The subjecting of a person to a second trial or punishment for the same offense for which the person has already been tried or punished

Due Process – The regular administration of the law, according to which no citizen may be denied his or her legal rights and all laws must conform to fundamental, accepted legal principles, as the right of the accused to confront his or her accusers

Eminent Domain – The power of the state to take private property for public use with payment of compensation to the owner

Fine – A sum of money exacted as a penalty by a court of law or other authority

Grand Jury – A jury, at common law, of twelve to twenty three persons, designated to inquire into alleged violations of the law in order to ascertain whether the evidence is sufficient to warrant trial

Human Rights – Fundamental rights, especially those believed to belong to an individual and in whose exercise a government may not interfere

Probable Cause – Reasonable ground for a belief that the accused was guilty of a crime

Self-Ownership – The condition by which an individual has the exclusive moral right to control his or her own body and life

Supreme Court – The highest federal court in the US, consisting of nine justices and taking judicial precedence over all other courts in the nation

Unconstitutional – Not constitutional; unauthorized by or inconsistent with the constitution, as of a country

Voluntaryism – The philosophy which holds that all forms of human association should be voluntary

Warrant – An instrument, issued by a judge, authorizing an officer to make an arrest, seize property, make a search, or carry a judgment into execution

About the author

Rory is a writer from Philadelphia, Pennsylvania, the Birthplace of Liberty.

His work has been featured with the Freedom Today Network, Speak Freely, Being Libertarian, and the Foundation for Economic Education.

His writing focuses on individual rights, peaceful dissidence, and American and Irish politics.

He currently resides in Phoenix, Arizona.

Made in the USA
Lexington, KY
05 May 2019